DEALING
WITH
DIFFICULT
PEOPLE

◆ ◆ ◆

PH EDITORIAL STAFF

PRENTICE HALL
Englewood Cliffs, NJ 07632

Prentice-Hall International (UK) Limited, *London*
Prentice-Hall of Australia Pty. Limited, *Sydney*
Prentice-Hall Canada, Inc., *Toronto*
Prentice-Hall Hispanoamericana, S. A., *Mexico*
Prentice-Hall of India Private Limited, *New Delhi*
Prentice-Hall of Japan, Inc., *Tokyo*
Simon & Schuster Asia Pte. Ltd., *Singapore*
Editora Prentice-Hall do Brasil, Ltda., *Rio de Janeiro*

© 1996 *by*
Prentice-Hall
Englewood Cliffs, NJ

10 9 8 7 6 5 4 3 2 1

Adapted from the following Prentice Hall titles:

Supervisor's Portable Answer Book, by George Fuller
What to Ask When You Don't Know What to Say, by Sam Deep and Lyle Sussman
Working with Difficult People, by Muriel Solomon

ISBN 0-13-472549-2

PRENTICE HALL
Englewood Cliffs, NJ 07632
A Simon & Schuster Company

PRINTED IN THE UNITED STATES OF AMERICA

CONTENTS

INTRODUCTION

Dealing with Difficult People

Difficult people. Sometimes it seems like you're surrounded by them.

- A subordinate openly challenges your directions on just about every job you assign to her, claiming that she has more experience than you do in that area or that you're trying to get her to do your work for you, or any other excuse she can come up with to undermine your authority.
- One of your colleagues is prone to fits of rage when he feels he's being pushed too hard; he's getting close to that point, and now you have to approach him about a project you're both supposed to be handling.
- You've found out that your boss has successfully implemented and taken full credit for an idea you suggested to him/her some weeks ago, at which time he/she brushed it aside as unworkable.

Anybody in the workplace who creates problems for others because of personality and attitude is a difficult person. No matter who you are, what you do, or where you work, chances are you encounter difficult people almost every day. Some are your subordinates, some are your co-workers, and some are your bosses. The way you handle these difficult people goes a long way toward determining how successful you will be at your job.

Anger, hurt, disappointment, and stress block your good judgment. Difficult people leave these kinds of feelings in their wake wherever they go. If you can recognize the kind of person you're dealing with and respond accordingly, using logic instead of emotion, you will be able to turn most bad situations to your advantage.

This is where *Dealing with Difficult People* comes in handy. First, we'll identify some of the worst types of difficult people from each category (subordinate, co-worker, boss). Then, we provide you with logical actions to take, proven methods for creating better relationships with the people at work who make your life miserable. By gaining their cooperation and respect, you'll be in complete control of even the most difficult workplace situation. You'll get what you want, when you want it—without stress and without tension.

PART I

Successfully Supervising Difficult People

The luck of the draw—in supervision as in life—means that you sometimes have to cope with problems you didn't bargain for. In a supervisory capacity, one of these unwelcome assignments is the misfortune of having to deal with difficult people.

Your roster of subordinates may include everything from gossips to goof-offs, know-it-alls to know-nothings, as well as folks who are just plain disagreeable. Such a wide array of personalities can mean handling hassles ranging from bad attitudes to employee theft. Since these kinds of problems are both time-consuming and stressful, it's worthwhile to explore ways of minimizing the damage that difficult workers can create.

FIVE POSITIVE WAYS TO COUNTERACT NEGATIVE ATTITUDES

One of the irritations of being a supervisor is having to contend with people who are constantly negative about their job in particular and the company in general. Rather than shrug your shoulders, however, it's important to try to modify their behavior, since negative attitudes can affect other employees. Here are five good ways to cope with bad attitudes:

1. **Be positive yourself.** By being essentially upbeat about matters, you can help to modify a negative attitude. Even if your good attitude doesn't have any impact on the "group grouch," it will encourage other employees to ignore the rumblings of a malcontent. This helps to maintain group loyalty and limit the spread of job dissatisfaction.

2. **Be a sounding board for complaints.** It's not pleasant to listen to gripes, but being a good listener pays dividends. Employees are going to air their gripes anyway, and if they feel at ease in doing so with you, they're less likely to grumble amongst themselves.

3. **Delegate responsibility.** Someone with a bad attitude isn't likely to change his or her behavior if he or she feels that what is bothersome can't be controlled. Therefore, if an employee is unhappy about some aspect of the job over which he or she has no influence, there's little hope for improvement. However, giving the person more responsibility in the troublesome area can help to eliminate the difficulty.

   For example, incorrect information in the office or defective parts on an assembly line can create real headaches for an employee. If the worker is given the authority to reject poor data or parts, however, that person won't be frustrated over having to live with someone else's mistakes. This can quickly turn a bad attitude around.

4. **Show respect.** It's easy when you're supervising someone who has a bad attitude to become tense and irritable when talking with the offender. Yet this just makes a bad situation worse. It can also influence other employees to form a judgment that the worker's bad attitude is attributable—at least in part—to your behavior. This may not be fair, but don't forget that you're the boss, so subordinates aren't going to judge your actions with a great deal of sympathy and/or objectivity. Therefore, it's important to be calm and matter-of-fact when confronted by people with bad attitudes.

5. **Be realistic.** If a bad attitude is caused by a job-related problem, do your best to resolve it. Having done that, however, you may find to your dismay that the person's attitude doesn't improve. If so, don't feel that you have failed. Attitudes are learned from others and can be formed over a long period of time. Furthermore, even when the attitude appears to be job-related, the root cause may be much deeper than that.

For instance, someone who has developed a deep-seated disrespect for authority over a lifetime isn't going to change that attitude overnight. Therefore, in some circumstances, the solution is simply to ignore a bad attitude. Naturally, this assumes that the worker is performing satisfactorily, without exerting a disruptive influence in the workplace.

LIGHTING A FIRE UNDER GOOF-OFFS

Goof-offs not only waste a lot of their own time but they can also require an inordinate amount of supervision. Everyone does a little goofing off from time to time, so concentrate your efforts on those few individuals who tend to slack off every time you turn your back.

Goof-offs come in several different forms. There are the obvious individuals who just aren't going to do any more work than the minimum required for survival, and survive they do for several reasons. First of all, some Goof-offs are quite clever at creating the illusion of being busy. In addition, some supervisors are reluctant to fire a dud. It's not unknown for Goof-offs to land a better job somewhere else, partly because of a glowing reference from their present employer. After all, it's a hassle-free way of unloading deadwood.

Other Goof-offs survive because of a mentor mentality that corrodes manager's minds. A supervisor who hires someone is often reluctant to admit a mistake or may just like the individual, so personal feelings cloud the fact that a buddy isn't hacking it.

Some incompetents survive by operating in obscurity. The best breeding ground for poor performers is often a large company where inadequacies either go unnoticed or are compensated for by other people.

Most people will do what they have to with a minimum of supervision, and a few will work hard whether or not you're around; but there are those who will seize every opportunity to avoid work. The first step in goof-off prevention is to make sure that people always have work to do. Some jobs have sharp peaks and valleys in their workload. A good supervisor will have low-priority tasks on the back burner to occupy people during slack periods.

Another less obvious reason that can encourage workers to goof off is a lax supervision. No one wants to be thought of as a tyrant, and a dictatorial boss can do much more harm than good. However, that doesn't mean you have to make everyone happy all of the time. A supervisor who constantly plays the role of "happy Harry" can be just as ineffective as a tyrant.

The bottom line is that you shouldn't worry about prodding Goof-offs. Happiness shouldn't be confused with productivity. Being firm—but fair—is what counts. Some workers need to be prodded more than others; therefore, don't worry about hurting feelings and alienating people who are goofing off. In fact, you may actually arouse resentment in subordinates who have to pick up the slack if you fail to make Goof-offs toe the line.

◆ ◆ ◆ **TIP:** If you have an employee who goofs off at every opportunity, try using what we'll call "progressive prodding" to get him going. A typical step-by-step procedure looks like this:

1. **Monitor the employee closely.** To eliminate the opportunity to goof off.
2. **Assign other work.** If the employee claims to have nothing to do, find other tasks. It's good to place a deadline for completion of these tasks, so time can serve as a motivator.
3. **Change the person's workload and/or work location.** Some jobs offer more opportunity for downtime than others. People who aren't self-starters are often better in positions that leave them little opportunity to slow down or to socialize.
4. **Confront the culprit.** Sit down with the employee and explain how much time is wasted and that you expect immediate improvement.
5. **Issue a formal warning.** If nothing else has succeeded, give the employee a formal warning in accordance with company policy. This should be a last resort, but once you start a step-by-step disciplinary action follow it through. Sometimes a stubborn worker doesn't get the message until a formal warning is given. Then he starts working when it hits home that his job is on the line.

GETTING BLAME SHIFTERS TO ACCEPT RESPONSIBILITY

Blame Shifters blame you for their own bonehead blunders. They are buck passers. Once they report a serious problem to you, it's your migraine; they've washed their hands of any further responsibility. When the anticipated disaster occurs, they have already transferred the sin to you, their scapegoat. It's all your fault.

Blame Shifters have difficulty handling pressure. If they feel criticized they have to relieve their hurt or fear or worry. So they remove the blame from themselves and hand it to you. You don't help them develop by promising to think about a matter they bring to you; that just saddles you with more worries about assignments that should have remained delegated.

Your goal is to get the Blame Shifters to accept responsibility for their own behavior. Start by reducing the emotional overload.

1. **Let them voice their anger or frustration.** Be empathetic, anxious to know what they think. Listen, without responding to the charges. Blame Shifters will try to make you their victims. Even if you contributed to a misunderstanding, that doesn't relieve them of their obligations.

2. **Suggest you meet soon.** You both need a little time to compose yourselves. Should the Blame Shifter's complaints be legitimate, you'll want to correct your action. When the atmosphere is calm again, start resolving the difficulty.

3. **Define the real problem.** Start by complimenting the Blame Shifter on specific matters handled well. Then point out the trouble spots. Keep the discussion impersonal.

4. **Don't do your subordinates' work for them.** Make them responsible for working on the solution and following through. Explain the consequences they face if they don't produce. Ask them to specify the tasks that have to be done and to set reasonable reporting deadlines. Now let go! There's a plan and a date; forget about the matter until then.

♦ ♦ ♦ **TIP:** Foil Blame Shifters who try to victimize you by handing you their mistakes and responsibilities. Don't contribute to their antics by promising to give them an answer later on. Help them by discussing the problem and let them suggest ways to handle it. Then stay on top of the matter through clearly defined reporting procedures.

WINNING THE CONTEST WHEN WORKERS PLAY GAMES

Some workers try to make careers out of challenging their supervisor at every opportunity. Instead of channeling their creativity into the job, they concentrate on testing your self-restraint.

The difficulty with Game Players is that they aren't as easy to control as other types of shirkers. They seemingly accept as a challenge any action you take. In fact, a worker skilled at playing games can go undetected for a considerable period of time. At other times, Game Players adopt an attitude of, "I'm yanking your chain. I know it and you know it, but you have to prove it."

Whereas Goof-offs and other shirkers are mainly trying to avoid work, the Game Player's focus is to challenge your authority. The kinds of games played are limited only by the imagination of the culprit. A few examples include

- **The on-the-job absentee.** There's always a reason for this character to be somewhere other than working. Such lines include, "I have to take this down to fabrication," or, "I wasn't late. I stopped off in Payroll to check on my vacation time."
- **The organization organizer.** Always takes up collections, organizes parties, or attends luncheons for someone leaving the company.
- **The working environment critic.** "It's too cold in here," which is quickly followed-up with a two-day absence with a cold, and a comment upon return, "I told you it was too cold in here. No wonder I got sick."
- **Self-promoters.** These people perform duties that they aren't authorized to do. If they get away with it, they'll later use this as a reason why they deserve a promotion. (This is one of the few instances where a Game Player does any work without being prodded.)
- **The boss knocker.** This type of person will contradict you in front of your boss, screw things up that you have to answer for—she has a ready-made excuse—and do anything else she can to make you look bad.

The long and the short of winning the battle with a Game Player is to lay it right on the line in a private meeting. Tell this person in so many words, "I know what you're up to, so don't think you're being cute." Naturally, she'll look shocked and adamantly deny what you're saying. Therefore, ignore her excuses, keep the meeting brief, and don't get drawn into a discussion with a glib Game Player who will just try to gloss over what you're saying. Once Game Players are directly confronted, they usually will (1) try to transfer within the company, (2) leave the company for another job, or (3) knock off the nonsense.

In the event the encounter doesn't have any impact, eventually you may have to take disciplinary action.

◆ ◆ ◆ **CAUTION:** Document deficiencies carefully, and keep your boss and personnel staffers informed as difficulties arise with Game Players. They tend to be experts at denial, so it's prudent to follow the rules carefully if you are forced to take formal action.

STRAIGHTENING OUT RULE BENDERS

Rule Benders cut corners, skirting the borders of acceptability. You don't need a search warrant to find these rebels. They're in plain sight. In their enthusiasm to get something done, these subordinates bend the rules almost to the breaking point or take unauthorized action and make their own rules as they go along. It doesn't matter whose turf they stomp on. They can be equally offensive to bosses and colleagues.

Some of them threaten you, demanding that you change your procedures or they won't produce what you desperately want. You find your spirit and self-respect held hostage as you try to get them to understand the importance of following your directives and getting along with others.

Your objectives are to get the Rule Benders to obtain permission before they attempt any unauthorized acts and, whenever possible, to maintain the go-getters' enthusiasm and productivity

1. **Reestablish universal rules and stick to them.** If you play the game with different sets of rules for certain players, you're inviting poor morale, possible sabotage, and even outright mutiny.

2. **Talk face-to-face with the Rule Bender.** Emphasize that (a) noncompliance is a serious problem for him, spelling out the serious consequences; (b) compliance is the Rule Bender's responsibility, getting him to tell you the exact steps he'll take to change his pattern; (c) his behavior is the focus of the discussion—what's acceptable and unacceptable. Praise what he does well, but don't let him off the hook with a claim that his ends justify his means.

3. **Follow up with feedback.** Be specific with your suggestions. Hopefully, you'll be able to tell him how well he's doing, acknowledging *any* improvement, and offering further suggestions.

♦ ♦ ♦ **TIP:** Be consistent in applying your regulations and in expecting adherence. If procedures need to be modified, change them. But if you give Rule Benders special privileges, you can expect other workers to feel resentful. Any semblance of team spirit will evaporate.

SNIFFING OUT SNEAKS

Some employees will take advantage of every opportunity to duck work. You can't spend your whole day trying to catch them in the act. So how do you maintain supervisory control over these difficult people?

There's no easy way to catch a Sneak, but there are adequate measures you can take that enable you to avoid time-consuming monitoring. In fact, the first mistake a supervisor can make is to engage in a sleuthing exercise. Sneaks aren't easily caught by following them around, and even when they are, you're only halfway home. That's because any Sneak worthy of the designation has a ready-made excuse in the event of being caught. Even after you think you've nabbed this person, you then will have to hurdle a rather ingenious alibi before you hang this person out to dry.

The best method of isolating and controlling the Sneak is two-pronged. The first is to be unpredictable in your movements. Sneaks are most successful when a manager follows a set pattern day in and day out. They then know when the boss will be in the office, goes to lunch, and in general, where and what the boss will be doing throughout the day. Counter this attempt to pinpoint your activities by randomly roaming the floor. You don't need to spend a lot of time doing this. The key to success isn't amount of time but rather the unpredictability of your actions.

The other tool of your two-pronged course of action is to forget about trying to catch the Sneak, since that can become a sophisticated game of hide-and-go-seek. As your participation becomes common knowledge, your subordinates may snicker at your efforts with a resultant loss of respect for you.

So instead of playing the Sneak's game, let her disappear and then leave her a note to see you. When she shows up, present her with a project to work on. After this is done a few times, the message will filter throughout the department.

Of course, you'll get the inevitable beef about doling out work like this. Nonchalantly toss these arguments aside with, "I checked with everyone else and they were busy. Unfortunately, you weren't here at the time so that left you as the only possibility." This off-hand turn of the screw will soon have Sneaks sticking around.

GETTING THE TRUTH OUT OF BLUFFERS

Bluffers are misleading fakers. They don't know and won't check it out. They conceal the truth or outright lie while giving you incomplete or wrong information. They palm off one thing as another, present data as accurate without bothering to verify, or assure you they've taken care of a matter when they have yet to lift a finger.

It may surprise you that some of these subordinates who lie, cheat, and snooker you are actually obsessive worriers who fear they can't handle the task and keep putting it off. Some Bluffers use stalling tactics because they're afraid that if they do what they're supposed to, they'll be trespassing on a cohort's turf.

Other Bluffers are lazy and irresponsible. A quirk in their personality makes them lie to get out of work. Some, out for revenge, invent work. They rip you off by creating problems that will require working overtime and thereby receiving overtime pay.

If you're being plagued by Bluffers, you probably have trouble "hearing" each other.

Your goal is to get everyone tuned into the same channel. Adjust the wavelength by

1. **Clarifying instructions.** You can eliminate a lot of bluffing/stalling by asking workers to restate assignments in their own words to be sure they understand. Talk about any concerns they may have. Shorten reporting periods with *segmented* deadlines. Assure the Bluffer who is also a perfectionist that he'll have time later to polish his masterpiece.

2. **Devising a better feedback plan.** This feedback should be more frequent, more specific, more helpful, and less threatening. With those you regard as irresponsible, keep the tone constructive instead of critical by concentrating on consequences rather than on threats.

3. **Linking individual performance to team spirit.** Act as though the Bluffer has already developed a potential capability you've detected. Talk in terms of the value of his work to the whole unit.

◆ ◆ ◆ **TIP:** Subordinates bluff for many reasons. More direct face-to-face communication will help allay their fears, have them believe you're on their side, and allow them to accept responsibility for their own actions.

CRAMPING THE STYLE OF CONSTANT COMPLAINERS

Have you ever told a subordinate, "I don't want to hear about it?" Even if you haven't mouthed the words, chances are that the thought has flashed through your mind on more than one occasion. Even though Chronic Complainers can engender these thoughts, it's not a good idea to shoot them down before you hear what they have to say.

A few helpful rules to follow are:

- **Always listen to complaints.** Even a Chronic Complainer may have a legitimate gripe.
- **Don't participate in gossip.** Doing so encourages workers to complain if they decide you have a willing ear.
- **Consider the complaint, not the complainer.** Is there a real basis for the complaint? If so, take the necessary steps to resolve it.
- **Pay particular attention to a noncomplainer.** When you get a gripe from someone who seldom complains it may signal a serious concern that needs attention.
- **Never minimize any complaint.** There may be more to it than meets the eye.

- **Be alert for situations that could escalate into complaints.** Take preventive measures if such a situation arises. For example, aggressive and alert supervisors can prevent sexual harassment or prejudicial behavior from developing by letting their people know it won't be tolerated.

- **Don't ignore general complaints about company policy.** Keep your boss informed when these gripes go beyond petty grumbling.

◆ ◆ ◆ **TIP:** No one wants to listen to complaints. You know this from your own life experiences apart from your job. Even if you are by nature a willing listener, the crush of daily duties doesn't allow the luxury of extensive hand-holding. Despite this, it's of vital importance to at least spend some time listening to even trivial complaints so workers know that you will listen to their concerns.

In fact, it's easy enough to discourage complaints by being harshly critical when you hear them. However, if you get to the point where you no longer get any complaints, you're either in utopia, or have discouraged subordinates from complaining. If it's utopia, try to recall if you recently received a sharp blow to the head, since you may need medical attention. Otherwise, start listening, since if you're not hearing occasional complaints, the chances are that you're out of touch with your subordinates. When that happens, disaster may be lurking in the wings.

DEFLATING A KNOW-IT-ALL

Know-It-Alls are never wrong in their own eyes, and seldom can be convinced otherwise. If you present them with facts that prove them wrong, they tend to shrug them off with an attitude of, "Don't confuse me with the facts." or "That wasn't what I said." If this sounds like someone you supervise, don't be surprised. Know-It-Alls in the world of work are as common as beer in a barroom.

How do you deal with an obnoxious Know-It-All who questions every decision you make and constantly belittles other workers?

Nothing teaches humility faster than hard work. Give the person the most undesirable tasks you can find—not the most technically difficult, but the most boring. If she challenges the assignment by saying something such as, "Why me? Any moron can do this job." you could avail yourself of the opportunity to say, "Then I'm sure you could handle it, Jennifer." But if you're kinder than that, just ignore the comment or tell her that's what she's paid for.

How can you tell the difference between a Know-It-All and someone who is just plain bright but perhaps not too diplomatic? The truly bright person will come up with good ideas that make sense. On the other hand, a Know-It-All will never admit to being wrong, and will usually claim expertise in everything except his own job.

At first blush, many Know-It-Alls are deceptive. They come across as intelligent, aggressive individuals, certainly characteristics that bode well for success. However, the very fact that a Know-It-All tries so hard to convince you of his wide-ranging knowledge is a warning. Following a Know-It-All's advice is a losing proposition, since he generally has difficulty distinguishing between what he really knows and what he thinks he knows.

Know-It-Alls are usually perceived to be snobs, and the reason is simple—they are. They see themselves as a cut above everyone else, and if they're not contained can cause a great deal of disharmony in the workplace.

◆ ◆ ◆ **TIP:** You might think that it would be better to give a Know-It-All all the most difficult tasks to solve, assuming, "If he's so smart, let him prove it." That's not a good idea for one reason. A Know-It-All will adopt an attitude of, "I was given this job because no one else can do it." But your objective isn't to further feed an overinflated ego; instead, it's to put some starch in his sails, and you do this by assigning him plenty of tedious, routine tasks.

COOLING OFF HOTHEADS

Hotheads are scrappers who start arguments among your workers. When Hotheads can't figure out how to cope with pressure, they can become belligerent. They provoke quarrels among their colleagues, but may not be angry at them. You may be seeing signs of their frustration because they have had to suppress their hostility. They may really be angry with you and are afraid to confront you.

Instructing them to stop worrying, or to relax, or that they ought to feel any given way won't diminish their hostility. It would help to get them to discuss their anger, but only if they trust you and believe they can talk to you about their feelings without risking their jobs.

Your objective is to keep your team from being disrupted. Help the Hothead articulate his anger and deal with it constructively so that he can become more productive.

1. **Review your management style.** Be sure you aren't rewarding nonperformance. When subordinates feel they are treated unfairly, great animosity can result. Establish your rules and periodically check yourself to see that you treat all your workers the same.
2. **Wait to discuss the problem.** Until your Hothead cools down, don't take a stand, just talk about the anger he's feeling. Then when he's able to tell you how he thinks he's being exploited, you can shift to solutions.
3. **Work together to resolve the issue.** Ask what he thinks would salve his injured feelings. Listen carefully, without interrupting. Nod agreement whenever you honestly can. When you disagree, ask more questions.

4. **Refuse to be a referee.** When two squabbling workers look to you to side with one of them, decide if the problem is in the system and something you can correct. If, for instance, others are putting too much pressure on them, monitor the work flow and route complaints through your desk. If there's a personality clash, insist they function as part of the team. Be firm, warning them that you won't tolerate interference with your standards and that if the disturbances continue, they'll both be gone.

♦ ♦ ♦ **TIP:** Sometimes you have to talk tough. If a subordinate threatens to quit unless you meet his demands, refuse the ultimatum and tell him you believe he's putting his interest above the company's and you can no longer bank on his loyalty. Usually, however, you can take a soft approach that will protect your Hothead's self-image and help him deal effectively with his hostility.

TURNING INSTIGATORS INTO PRODUCTIVE WORKERS

Instigators are troublemakers. They stir up other workers and provoke action. These subordinates say nasty things, twisting the truth to goad other workers, fomenting unnecessary problems. While they don't steal equipment or supplies, they are guilty of stealing your time. You have to keep putting out the brush fires their prodding has initiated.

Some Instigators are bored, unchallenged, underutilized high achievers. It could be a mismatch of job and worker. Or, they see no reason for assignments they find unexciting and unimportant, and they know they're capable of doing a lot more.

Some Instigators are expressing their resentment of your management style. If you keep stressing what they do wrong, they may be pleading for personal growth opportunities. Or they want to get back at you for chewing them out, throwing cold water on their hot ideas, or making it impossible for them to penetrate a tight circle of select employees. Also, they might be having personal problems and are taking out their hostility on you.

Other Instigators rebel against the red tape that stifles any initiative. Some have been disillusioned by phoniness and resent compromises that occur in the workplace. They've been hurt and want to expose acts they consider unfair or unethical because they still care deeply about integrity.

Your goal is to turn troublemakers around and help reshape their destructive efforts into productive ones.

1. **Add excitement to reduce the mischief.** When feasible, rotate jobs for the joy and value of learning something new. Start competition among your units, with meaningful prizes as a reward. Discover the one thing a

low achiever desires (everyone wants something) and encourage him to go after it.

2. **Show your understanding.** Let workers know you feel some affinity for their position because you were once in their shoes. Explore without trying to trap. Suggest training courses that could help them achieve personal goals. Enlarge the circle of people you listen to. Show your confidence in them by planning meetings, workshops, and informal sessions to garner their ideas. Double-check your personnel policies to assure fair and equal treatment.

3. **Give the Instigator more control over his own work.** Eliminate overly restrictive rules requiring ten signatures before he can act. Explain why the company is moving in a given direction, then give him a chance to buy into your ideas. Let rebels become creative by designing a plan and implementing it once it has your approval. Share, delegate, and eliminate excessive superstructure.

♦ ♦ ♦ **TIP:** Instigators cause trouble because they feel bored, bitter, or restricted. Review your rules, policies, and procedures to add excitement, understanding, and opportunity. Especially, eliminate the extraneous to make room for the spontaneous.

HANDLING RUMORMONGERS

Rumormongers are gossips who spread unverified facts of questionable origin. Their intent is to gain attention for themselves by aggrandizing untrue or partly true messages. They often embroider the story, filling in the blanks to make it appear more important or believable, or to sound like they think it "should." They may go the other way, forgetting details, remembering only vivid parts and distorting the facts by omitting vital information. Rumormongers interpret what happened or is about to happen based on their own interests. Their own experiences, expectations, and views color and limit how they report a situation.

The difficulty for you is deciding which story or how much of a story to believe.

You never know if a Rumormonger is telling a story that is true, partly true, or entirely false. Your goal is to listen and sift information for parts that can be verified and, if necessary, acted upon.

1. **Keep your door open.** Let the Rumormonger come in and talk to you. You want to hear about problems that can affect your operation before everybody else does.

2. **Cut short discussions that are obviously meaningless and spiteful gossip.** Respond in a disinterested, noncommittal manner.

3. **Ask a lot of questions of the Rumor Monger.** Try to find out where the story originated and how reliable the information is. Determine if this is a firsthand or seventhhand account.

4. **Check the facts.** How much is true and how much has been distorted? What are the dangers of acting—or not acting—on this information immediately?

♦ ♦ ♦ **TIP:** You can listen to the Rumormonger without condoning idle gossip. It's important to keep your ear to the ground and find out what is going on that might influence your part of the world. But as with any rumor, you have to trace it, verify it, and deal with the reality.

BAILING OUT GRACEFULLY WHEN YOU'RE BEING BAITED

Some people delight in baiting others. If such a person works for you, it can be pretty annoying. However, in most cases it's relatively harmless—unless of course, you lose your cool and rise to the bait.

For example, you may have subordinates who needle you with comments like, "How come the people in Accounting get to leave early on Fridays?" or "Why do Production workers get 9 percent raises when we only get 5 percent?"

If you want to avoid being baited, you have to learn to refuse to bite the bait. Although it's important to communicate effectively with workers and to argue on their behalf when necessary, there are limits. That means you can't spin your wheels chasing down every gripe to sort out fact from fiction. By doing so, you open yourself up for continuous baiting. It's possible to get inadvertently drawn into this trap if you're conscientious about checking out employee questions. However, you have to be careful to separate the real concerns from the nonsense.

A sure sign that you're going overboard is if you chase around knocking down allegations such as those posed above. If that's happening, rein yourself in. That requires giving short-shrift to endless comparisons with other departments. Once you start saying, "That's nonsense," and/or "Don't worry about other people," the baiting will subside.

CONFRONTING DEFIERS

Defiers are insubordinate and disrespectfully oppose established policy. You give an order to some subordinates and they won't do it, don't do it, or delay doing it. They meet each and every assignment by confronting, resisting, challenging, and daring you to do something about their defiance. Eventually the work gets done, but you're worn out from the battle.

Your objective is to get peak performances from all your workers. You want to be reasonable with each one while you keep your eye on the big picture. Your vantage point is not available to your subordinates unless you explain to them how it looks from where you sit.

1. **Check your own attitude.** When a worker is defiant, ask yourself if you're being open and playing fair. Do you request or command adherence? Are you explaining the importance of doing something a certain way? Do you turn mistakes into learning experiences for both of you? Do you resist dangling promises unless you're sure you can keep them?

2. **Get right to the point of your meeting.** Don't beat around the bush or make small talk. Immediately put your subordinate at ease by expressing your desire to continue your working relationship.

3. **Let the defiant worker get his gripe off his chest.** Listen carefully, then bend where you can, but explain why certain procedures must be followed. In a calm, professional manner, ask him to explain why he deliberately disobeyed a directive. Get him to tell you the probable consequences of such actions. Ask him how he plans to deal with the situation.

♦ ♦ ♦ **TIP:** A subordinate working on one segment of the operation can't have the same global picture as his boss, who's supervising the whole show. While workers' views are invaluable and need to be discussed in group meetings, and while workers have to be free to complain to you, it's still up to you to enforce company policy and important procedures. If you are tactful, both you and your defiant subordinate will feel you won something in the discussion.

REINING IN PRIMA DONNAS

Prima Donnas are temperamental workers, demanding that you give them special treatment. Often conceited and vain performers, Prima Donnas have a way of intimidating and manipulating you into believing the company will fold without them. We can speculate that they were spoiled as children and learned early how to get others to do their work for them. They aren't lazy, but they are shrewd. They use many tricks, such as issuing ultimatums, to get special attention. In return for certain demands, they dangle prizes you long for, such as promising to introduce you to decision makers who can close a deal. Generally, Prima Donnas are moody and have short fuses. The danger is that they wear down your resistance.

Your objective is to maintain control by guiding the Prima Donna to act more responsibly.

1. **Call her bluff.** Stop acting intimidated and allowing the Prima Donna to interfere with your operation. Whatever the Prima Donna has that you want, it's better to do without it than have her usurp your authority and destroy team spirit.

2. **Help her become part of the team.** Be friendly but very firm in insisting that your procedures be followed. If you want your whole group pulling together, you have to treat each one the same way. Also, you can enlist the support of the Prima Donna's peers to apply pressure on her to join in.

◆ ◆ ◆ **TIP:** Recognize the games that Prima Donnas play. Like children who pout, stamp their feet, and throw tantrums, they use a variety of irritating techniques to wear you down and get their own way. You have to reinforce your rules and stick to them.

P A R T   I I

Dealing with Difficult Co-workers

Many of us work more closely on a daily basis with our co-workers than with either our superiors or our subordinates. These peers have a profound influence on both our job satisfaction and our job performance. When they cooperate, we succeed; when they undermine our efforts, we may fail.

It's tough to give feedback to colleagues when their behavior puts us on the spot. They do not report to us, and they consider themselves our equals. In most cases, talking things out with a difficult co-worker is the only way to reach some level of understanding and cooperation. You will find that questions are especially valuable when dealing with people at your own level. Questions enable you to make important points without appearing to take a superior position. And by opening co-workers up to constructive feedback, questions set the stage for getting your ideas across.

WORKING HAND-IN-HAND WITH COMPETITORS

Competitors feel the need to surpass you, making the simplest contest a rivalry. Some pushy/presumptuous colleagues push competition beyond its intended purpose. Not only must they win standard organized matches such as sales contests, they also attempt to turn most other tasks into a clash purely for the "prize" of coming out ahead. You can be brainstorming for a solution, everybody offering possibilities, and only the Competitor takes it as a personal rejection when his idea isn't accepted. By denying him the applause he seeks, you become his enemy.

You aren't aware you're in a contest while Competitors feel compelled to keep winning at whatever they do with you, regardless of what it costs them. Deep down, they are afraid they aren't really excelling, and so they feel forced to prove to themselves and to you that they are superior. They are saddled with an unnecessary load—the feat that they may not continue being the best.

Competitors are on top of the world when they win; in the dumps when they don't. All this subjects you to a perpetually tense situation.

Your goal is to help restore a friendly climate. To enjoy your work without feeling the hot breath of hostility:

1. **Be professional and gracious.** Give the Competitor the respect and recognition he desperately seeks. In a professional manner, show him you want to be friends even though he rebuffs you. Allow him to feel important so that he won't have to run you down in order to uplift his self-esteem.

2. **Explain the value of synthesizing.** The whole (the resulting outcome) is greater than the sum of the parts because when you share your thinking and extract the best thoughts from each of you, you form a new and more valuable combination.

3. **Be honorable in taking and giving credit.** You want credit for your work, and the Competitor should get credit for his. Don't allow anyone to claim as *his* achievement your efforts or joint efforts. Concentrate on running your own race—no seeking revenge with dirty tricks or backstabbing.

4. **Be up front.** Inform your colleague if you're going to compete for a job opening or assignment that you know he's hoping to get. It will get back to him anyway if you talk, for example, to the personnel director. Expect it to be common knowledge around the office before you get back to your desk. And when the competition is over, regardless of who won, take steps to mend any rift. You can remain friendly rivals. Neither of you needs bitter enemies.

Questions to Ask

Can we agree to replace the win-lose parts of our relationship with win-win? If your boss does not recognize the problem of competitive employees, you have to take matters into your own hands. Expect this question to elicit, "Certainly" or "What do you mean?" Respond by describing the positive behavior you expect in situations where, in the past, you've been deceptively outdone. Focus on the positive of what you want to see rather than on the negative of what you've been seeing.

If, instead, the answer to the question is something like, "Not if that means you expect me to kiss your feet," you're in trouble. All you can do is get help from other co-workers or from your boss, or appeal to the person's desire to avoid declared war with you.

Before you ask *any* questions of the other person, ask these of yourself. Is there any chance that you contribute to a competitive environment in your office? Do you give others reason to feel threatened? Do you show off yourself?

What benefit did you get out of leaving my name off the annual report? Notice how much more powerful this question is than, "Why did you leave my name off the annual report?" It helps keep the focus on the act rather than making it easy for the other person to deflect the issue.

Be prepared to defeat any rationale proposed for the omission. If the person claims an oversight, say, "Then I'm certain you won't mind issuing a notice to that effect to recipients of the report. I'll draft it for your signature."

If the answer is a blunt, "I didn't feel your name deserved to be on it." your only recourse may be to bring the situation to your boss. Take care, however, not to be seen as a whiner. Make a straightforward statement of what happened, what damage you believe was caused, and any remedies you would like the boss to help you pursue.

♦ ♦ ♦ **TIP:** If your own ego is intact, you can afford to be generous. You can give your Competitor-cohort the reassurance he needs while you are spurred on to greater creativity, matching wits with someone else who's reaching for a better way.

DODGING THE TACKLERS

Tacklers attack you personally while arguing an issue. These colleagues are so determined to score points with the boss that they block whatever you toss out for consideration and tackle you instead of the problem. They twist everything you say so that you become the opponent who has to be brought down and overcome.

When they tackle you, you know you've been hit. They don't hold back with their attack. You feel hurt, but are more concerned with the consequences. Your credibility is being kicked around like a football. How can you keep the Tacklers from injuring your career?

Your goal is to maintain your professionalism as you carry out your assignments, while minimizing any damage the Tackler can do to your standing.

1. **Continue your game plan.** Don't be sidelined by a groveling match. Instead, question the Tackler to show that you are determined to do the job without stooping to his level. Elevate the discussion by moving the emphasis away from individuals and back to the issue at hand.

2. **Talk to him privately if he continues to tackle you.** Say that you'd like to have a better relationship and ask how he thinks you might be able to resolve your differences.

3. **Learn where you can—and can't—expect support.** Determine through the grapevine if the Tackler has company friends in high places. If so, an ongoing feud could hurt your chance to advance. It's not worth the fuss. Concentrate on doing your job and making more friends.

Questions to Ask

Are you aware of the injustice you caused in our staff meeting this morning? If the answer is a quizzical no, you have created a perfect opening to give the feedback you are just dying to deliver. If it's something like, "Are you referring to my comment about personal distractions?" or if the person denies demeaning you or apologizes, deliver the feedback anyway.

In criticizing the Tackler's act, report exactly what was said as well as what you saw or heard in response to it; in other words, how what was said created a problem. Then document the inaccuracy of the statement as it relates to your work and state how you feel about what was said. Finally, ask for commitment to the precise behavior you expect to observe in similar future situations. Throughout be as factual, unemotional, and nonpunishing as possible.

Ask yourself why you think this happened. It will help to be as analytical and objective as possible about your co-worker's motives. Are this person's comments frequently punishing, possibly discounted by others, and therefore not worthy of response? Finally, how much truth may there be in what was said?

What evidence do you have that my personal matters are delaying the project? If the answer is no evidence, ask that a retraction be made to the boss. Even though you are not likely to get one, this notifies the person that you are likely to be alert and instantly protective at repeat performances.

If you receive a denial that the reference in the meeting was about you, indicate your rejection of the denial and insist on more professional behavior in the future. Add your opinion that the unfortunate statement was an equally unflattering reflection on the perpetrator.

Finally, in case your co-worker answers with so-called evidence, be prepared to discredit it rationally and calmly. It won't help to become defensive or to counterattack.

Do you believe that coworkers should pull each other down in front of the boss? The wisest response would be something such as, "When we see something wrong, we have an obligation to point that out even if it embarrasses the wrongdoer." Agree completely with this statement, but add that there are two times you wouldn't do it. One is when the embarrassment outweighs the value of a public airing of the problem, in which case you would opt for a private disclosure to the boss. The other is when you didn't know what you were talking about. Make it very clear that *this* was the case in the staff meeting.

◆ ◆ ◆ **TIP:** You're not after 100-percent harmony. You and your Tackler will seldom sing the same tune. You just need to come to some understanding that lets you get on with your work. To arrange a truce, handle the conflict with direct, clear, face-to-face confrontation instead of memos or phone calls, which may tend to muddy the waters.

PROTECTING YOURSELF FROM BRAINPICKERS

Brainpickers exploit your ideas, stealing credit for and profiting from them. Brainpickers are phony office friends who pretend to care about you, but only care about information they can extract from you. Instead of suggesting that you team up and brainstorm some idea or activity to which you both contribute and claim credit, they probe your mind with delicately worded questions. Then they take your brainchild and adopt it or adapt it as their own.

You thought that once you left the street and entered the office you were safe from thieves? Just as pickpockets steal your wallet, Brainpickers steal your ideas. Because these con artists don't use guns, you don't even know you were being robbed.

Obviously, you won't gain anything from a confrontation. The Brainpicker has already convinced himself that your ideas came to him as divine inspiration. Learn from your mistake. Your objective now is to separate your concepts into those you want to present as your own proposals and those that need the collective wisdom of a group to be properly developed. Then direct the flow of your ideas.

1. **Plug the leak.** Once you've fingered the folks who want to drain your brain, be polite but tight-lipped. Just stop supplying the information.
2. **Welcome discussion when concepts affect other units.** You don't want to work in a vacuum, not when you need the cooperation of your cohorts. But don't limit yourself to a one-Brainpicker audience. Enlarge the group. Call over other colleagues or bring up these matters at lunch or at staff meetings.

Questions to Ask

Where did you get that idea? The answer to this question will determine how you open your discussion of the "theft," but the ultimate thrust of your censure will be the same no matter what the answer. (Of course, the person may somehow convince you that she developed this idea before you did and that your conversation with her merely convinced her to come forward with it.)

With your response, let her know how you feel about plagiarism, especially when one of your ideas is presented to the boss by someone else claiming credit for it. Before you confront this person, decide exactly what you expect as a remedy, and then demand it.

Should you or should I tell the boss where the idea came from? Unless your idea-stealing colleague is willing to negotiate reparations to your satisfaction, this is the ultimate question. Make it clear that you intend to tell the boss exactly what happened with or without her present. Unless she believes that she has more legitimacy with the boss than you do and is planning to engage in the "big lie" strategy, this should cause her to retreat.

This question is a forceful assertion of your anger, your rights, and your expectation for redress. You're telling the person in unequivocal terms that the boss will be told, either by you or by her.

If you sense that the person is experiencing sincere remorse and is worried about being fired, you have two options. The first is to demand the credit you deserve. Choose this if you think the person is playing you for a sucker or if you believe that the deserved kudos are necessary for your career mobility. The second option is to pull back and allow the person to save face. You might choose this if the person manifests sincere regret or if you believe the job of victory is not worth the pain of battle.

Is there any reason why I should not go to the boss right now to set the record straight? The preceding question conveyed your moral indignation and demanded a remedy. This question implies that you night be convinced otherwise. There are at least two predictable responses to your question. The first is for your co-worker to defend her claim to the idea successfully, in which case you'll want to gracefully back down. The second is for your co-worker to come clean, apologize, and seek your forgiveness. If you can forgive and forget, do so; you'll prove that you're the bigger person. Holding a grudge can rob you of energy better spent on more productive tasks.

If you were in my shoes right now, what would you do? This powerful question solicits empathy and role reversal. Borrowing a co-worker's ideas and presenting them as one's own often occurs without thought of repercussions or of the pain it may cause the true originator of the idea. With this question you're implying that there is pain and you want her to describe it.

If she can't empathize or refuses to do so, tell her *exactly* how you are feeling and exactly what you plan to do as a result.

♦ ♦ ♦ **TIP:**   OK, you were snookered by the Brainpicker. Be glad this happened to you now. You'll be wiser in the future when you come up with a really brilliant gem. Then you'll know how to nourish, protect, and present your prize-winning idea.

WATCHING OUT FOR BACK-STABBERS

Back-Stabbers are nice to your face, but very critical of you behind your back. These colleagues stab you *in absentia*. They are bad-mouthers, telling lies or being critical about you when you're not there. When you're with them, they act like they're your friends. But out of sight, the phonies betray your trust, revealing some disclosure you made about your personal life or opposing some action you've taken.

They keep trying to outwit you or get some measure of control over you. Maybe they misinterpreted your action. Maybe you did something that angered them, but you can't imagine what it was. You're scratching your head while you're pulling the blade out of your back.

Your objective is to stop the back-stabbing. If criticism of your work is legitimate, that has to be aired and resolved.

1. **Confront the Back-Stabber.** Simply report what you heard. Don't start swinging. Ask her to spell out specifically whatever accusations she allegedly made. Speak up firmly, without showing any anger or voicing any blame.

2. **If the mistake was yours, apologize immediately.** Sometimes you become a victim of a Back-stabber if she perceives you were insensitive to her feelings. If, for example, she believes that you meant to put her down by elevating yourself, you could have made her feel insecure and want to strike back at you.

3. **Provide a graceful way out.** If the Back-stabber accuses you unjustly and then denies having made the reported statements, let her off the hook. Once she knows that you know she's attacked your reputation and you won't sit still for such immature behavior, the Back-stabber will back off. But if you create an emotional scene, a tip-off that she got a rise out of you, she may keep it up.

Questions to Ask

Believing a co-worker's lies, your boss just accused you of something for which you share no blame. You listened carefully to the boss's complaint without interrupting to make certain that you understood it and to muster a succinct response.

May I take a few minutes to reveal some information about this situation that you should have? It won't help to accuse your criticizer of being unfair, even if that's the case. Rather, you want the boss to remain open to the possibility that the discipline was unwarranted. Turn the focus to the situation that generated the remarks. First confirm the agreement you have with her reading of the situation. Then politely, yet firmly, correct any inaccurate information given by the criticizer. Say what you saw and what happened. Report the situation as objectively as you can. Don't get caught in embellishments or lies that will permanently damage your credibility. Thank the boss for the opportunity to share your perception. Don't blame the co-worker who smeared you. Let the boss do that.

How do you want me to handle this in the future? If you are really not a fault, you'll be able to respond to your boss's answer to this question by saying, "That's exactly what I did," and then elaborate on the situation as it happened. You can help to further discredit the perjured witness by ending with, "You may have received some bad information from someone."

◆ ◆ ◆ **TIP:** If you allow the back-stabbing to persist, it can eventually harm your reputation. Back-stabbing is childish. And it takes your calm, nononsense demeanor to make the culprit behave as an adult.

STEERING CLEAR OF IMPOSERS

Imposers take unfair advantage of your time, talent, and good nature. Colleagues such as these are just plain self-centered and inconsiderate of others. You certainly don't mind doing a favor every once in a while, and you're glad to pitch in during an emergency, but Imposers make a habit of exploiting you. They are so wound up in whatever they want to do that they are oblivious to anyone else's feelings or needs. They promise to return the favor and never do, but you're not looking for favors. You want them to leave you alone and stop saying that you ought to help them "because that's what friends are for." No friend would be that unfeeling and presumptuous.

Some Imposers put on a helpless act. These poor dependent souls aren't helpless at all, just crafty in getting you to do their work while they use company time for personal business.

You know that what they're doing is wrong. You hate being a part of it, but you don't want to hurt their feelings. You have great difficulty saying no to Imposers.

Your goal is to free yourself from doing something you don't want to do. This is especially important if you also believe what you've been asked to do is wrong and you feel torn between helping a colleague and obeying company policy.

1. **Remember that you really don't need a reason to refuse a request.** Expressing your regret is sufficient. But if that sticks in your soft-hearted throat, sandwich your refusal between two compliments or helpful comments.

2. **Practice firm responses at home.** Listen to yourself on a tape recorder. Or role-play rejections so that they roll off your tongue in a calm and polite manner. Just because you think your colleague is being lazy or inconsiderate doesn't give you the right to be rude.

3. **Suggest more appropriate ways to deal with the problem.** Consider how else the needs of the Imposer might be met in a more responsible fashion. Place that responsibility back where it belongs—on the Imposer—without showing signs of hostility or sarcasm.

Questions to Ask

May I first help you figure out what's preventing you from staying on top of your workload?   This question is preferable either to saying no (making you look uncooperative) or saying yes (making you this person's dupe). Stated as above, it implies that you might pitch in but only after confronting the reasons for your colleague's lack of productivity. If you wish to make the question more powerful and perhaps off-putting, change "first" to "instead" or follow "of" with "a workload that's no greater than mine." Decide what wording works best for you.

Expect one of two responses. "Never mind!" or something similar means that you've successfully put the person on notice that you're no patsy. A more inquisitive retort ("What makes you so hostile?") may give you the opportunity to say how you feel about the person's behavior and to document the impact it has on you.

What prevents you from doing it yourself?   This is less cooperative than the original question. You'll want to reserve it for chronic deadweights. There's a slim chance you'll hear a tale of woe that justifies the request. If you do, offer whatever help you choose.

More likely, the answer to this question will allow you to give direct and specific feedback to your co-worker on the behavior that you feel causes him to ask you for help. You'll also want to add a few words describing the ferocity of your own workload.

◆ ◆ ◆ **TIP:**   Refuse to be used. You're not really helping dependent people by supplying a crutch instead of making them face their responsibilities. And you're not helping yourself by remaining silent when you're being unreasonably imposed upon. If you're meek and don't speak, you won't like yourself. The anger within you will build and eventually explode, and then you'll find yourself apologizing to peers, friends, and family. Speak up!

DISRUPTING THE INTERRUPTERS

Interrupters rudely break into your discussion, burst into your office uninvited, or pester you on the phone. What is most irritaking about Interrupters is that they nibble away at your peak productive hours. They plop down at your desk during the time you had set aside to plot a potentially big project. After they leave or you finish their calls, you can't recapture the thoughts that were interrupted. Almost as annoying is when they waste your time at meetings by getting the discussion off the track. They speak in stage whispers to fellow workers when you're trying to hear the boss's comments on the latest marketing report. They never let you finish the point you're making.

Usually, Interrupters don't know they are regarded as pests or long-winded bores. Their crime is being self-centered and inconsiderate. Their punishment, eventually, is being ignored. In the meantime your stress level is climbing to the breaking point.

Your aim is to break your colleague's thoughtless behavior pattern. To do so you have to interrupt the Interrupter. But handle with care or your Interrupter will become antagonistic, possibly leading to other problems.

1. **Be polite when you do the interrupting.** Smile, address the person by name, and couple your friendly tone with sensitive phrases. Be considerate even though your Interrupter is not.

2. **Be straightforward in explaining why you can't be interrupted now.** People understand when you're under pressure. You don't need phony gimmicks, such as knocking on your desk, in order to fib to the telephone caller that someone's waiting for you. Just explain that you have a deadline, a report to prepare, or preconference materials to gather. If you don't have time to talk right then but want to continue, suggest a time that's mutually convenient.

3. **Snatch back control when your conversation is intercepted.** Interrupt your Interrupter for a minute or two to finish making your point.

4. **Stop the rambler with sharply focused comments and questions.** Bring the discussion back to the stated purpose. Politely break in to summarize an Interrupter's unending monologue.

5. **Discourage Interrupters from coming in and staying in your office.** Reposition your desk so that passersby can't catch your eye. Limit the number of chairs or stack them with reports or phone books. Stand up when an Interrupter comes in and remain standing.

Questions to Ask

May we make an appointment to get together tomorrow?   If the person is already in overdrive, you'll need to break in both assertively and positively with this question. The answer is likely to be, "Sure. Why?" Then you can say, "Because this deadline I'm working on today needs every minute I have." Immediately look at your calendar for a time that you can afford to offer. Chances are good that the person will say something like, "That's okay, don't bother. It's not that important." Smile and say something like, "See you later" in a pleasant voice.

If you wish to be less solicitous, replace the question with a statement about your unrelenting workload and ask for a postponement of the visit.

Whether you ask a question or make a statement, thank the person on the way out.

May I finish what I'm working on before we talk?   The implication of this question is that the person may hang around until you finish what you're doing. If he does, keep your eyes on the job without engaging in conversation, and the person will usually leave within a few minutes. If not, you can state after a while, "This is getting a lot more involved than I thought. I'm afraid I'll have to accept a raincheck from you."

Alternatively, you may hear, "That's all right. I'll come back later when you're not so busy." Mission accomplished!

If the Interrupter objects with something such as, "This is really important" and you give in, you have at least notified your co-worker to be brief.

May I ask you to come back later when I'm not as busy?   More than the previous two questions, this one shoos the person out of your office. Use it when your work comes before any consideration of the other person's needs. Even so, notice that it does leave a crack open for the assertive person to ask for an exception.

◆ ◆ ◆ **TIP:**   Interrupters either are not aware or do not care that they are selfishly imposing their needs on others. You can refuse to accept this form of rudeness and yet be gracious yourself. So if you're being interrupted and can't think of what to say, remember George Bernard Shaw's observation: "Silence is the most perfect expression of scorn."

SHUTTING THE DOOR ON SNOOPS

Snoops are unduly inquisitive, prying when it's none of their business. Seldom do they realize how offensive their questions and actions actually can be. Curiosity is admirable when one is doing legitimate research, but these peers dig for data like they're preparing a feature story for the *National Tattler*.

They act as though the information in your confidential files or about your private life ought to be public information that they, if not the entire public, have a right to know.

Their curiosity *has* to be satisfied. Not content with impertinent or presumptuous questions, they also wait for you in your office, while reading through your files. Don't worry so much about hurting their feelings; they're usually too insensitive to be hurt.

You probably can't stop the Snoop from being so snoopy, but you can aim to stop him from prying inappropriate information out of you. What's more, you can do this without sounding rude or antagonistic.

1. **Give him the benefit of the doubt.** Act as though the Snoop doesn't know he is asking for information that is too personal or confidential to reveal.

2. **Remember that just because someone asks, you don't have to answer.** Briefly explain why giving away such information would be inappropriate. If you can pull it off with a smile on your face, you could even ask him why he wants to know.

Questions to Ask

Snoops regularly pry into your area of responsibility. Questions about how your work is proceeding have nothing to do with concern for your welfare, nor does your progress affect theirs in any way.

Would you like to do it for me?   This question is an indirectly assertive and powerful way of saying, "Stay out of my business." It is preferable to that, especially if stated nonantagonistically, because it is not defensive and puts the other person on notice.

The answer is likely to be a surprised no that you can acknowledge with "Good." You can immediately continue with what you were doing prior to the intrusion. In the unlikely case that you invoke a yes, be prepared either to subcontract part of your work or to state firmly that although you appreciate the offer, you intend to complete the job yourself.

Why do you ask?   This is another powerful but polite way to say, "Buzz off." It immediately focuses on the legitimacy of the Snoop's inquiry. If he has a good reason to ask about your progress, acknowledge that and give the appropriate status report. If instead he's out of line, this question should make him feel that way.

Do you think I should be finished with it?   This question is likely to surprise and confuse your nosy co-worker. If he says yes, you respond, "Well, that shows how little you know about my responsibilities and the quality of results I'm looking for. Perhaps you should keep your mind on your own job."

If he says no, say, "Good. I was worried about you for a minute."

◆ ◆ ◆ **TIP:** You are under no obligation to answer queries that are too personal. To soften a refusal you can say you can't answer because that would be violating a confidence. You can politely stop the Snoop you find reading your mail as you return to your office. Smile as you ask, "Hi, Matt, what can I help you find?"

STANDING UP TO KNOW-IT-ALLS

Know-It-Alls are smart alecks, arrogantly claiming to know everything about everything. Bursting with self-confidence, Know-It-Alls are obnoxious extroverts who cram their opinions down your throat. Masters at promoting themselves, these colleagues usually know a great deal, as opposed to Bluffers, who only pretend to be well informed.

Know-It-Alls flaunt their intelligence, with their vanity shining through every line. Because they are competent, efficient, and thorough planners who cover all the angles, they have little use for your input and no tolerance if you subject their opinionated statements to debate.

Since Know-It-Alls are usually right, your goal is to extract and utilize the clever thoughts that make them crow without letting their words stick in your craw.

1. **Listen carefully to formulate good questions.** Don't interrupt with counterarguments but with strong, solid questions. Ask, for example, how this compares, what results have been reported, over what period of time, what resources are required.

2. **Do your own homework.** Verify the information. If you think Know-It-Alls are wrong, matter-of-factly present contradictory data. Don't directly challenge their expertise, but suggest another way to view the situation.

Questions to Ask

A Know-It-All has always warned you to check up more on the work of your employees. You've continually responded with your philosophy of empowering employees by giving them greater responsibility for their jobs and greater discretion in how they perform them. One of your employees was fired today for stealing from the company over the past year. The employee was so devious that no controls could have either prevented the thefts or uncovered them before now. But now the Know-It-All co-worker is in your office saying, "I told you so!"

What was it that you told me?   The answer will almost certainly be, "That you weren't keeping a close enough eye on your employees." Here are two suggested responses. First, describe how well all your employees flourish under your leadership style and give specific examples of the productivity you're getting because of the treatment you give your workers. Second, launch into the following questions.

Would you like to hear the story of what really happened in this situation?   If the Know-It-All doesn't want to hear the explanation, say something like, "Then please leave. I have more important things to do than to provide a forum for your childish gloating."

If the person is willing to listen, share just enough of the situation to emphasize that no amount of practical controls could have prevented the problem. If the theft involves the slightest potential for future legal action, reveal no details beyond what your colleague needs to know.

What value do you find in saying that to me?   You hope this question will put the Know-It-All in her place. If so, and if she says, "No particular value," respond with, "Then why did you say it?"

If she mumbles something defensively, tell her that you disagree and why. Point out that her statement was nothing more than an attempted insult. Add that it does nothing to strengthen your relationship or to improve the ability to work together productively.

♦ ♦ ♦ **TIP:** Know-It-Alls are bright and usually right. On those occasions you're sure they're wrong, if you try a frontal attack or back them into a corner, Know-It-Alls will bombard you with a fusillade of irrelevant data to support their position. They consider any opposition a personal affront. The only way to quiet them is to offer them a gracious way to save face.

P A R T   I I I

Bearing Up Under Difficult Bosses

Just as you have a considerable amount of control over the success or failure of your subordinates, your boss holds similar power over you. That presents a real challenge, since for the most part you can't choose a boss, so you're stuck with what you get, for better, if you handle it right; or for worse, if you don't.

Frequently, folks grumble and moan about their boss, all too often forgetting that the key to success is learning how to manage a boss, much as you strive to manage your subordinates—although from a different perspective.

LEARNING HOW THE BOSS PLAYS OFFICE POLITICS

Although most managers practice some degree of social diplomacy, the Politicians of the working world consider it to be the solitary path to success. In fact, they may, at least partially, owe their job to the use of ego-flattering techniques. From your vantage point, it's vital to be aware of how significant the game of office politics is to your boss's agenda.

Certain bosses play office politics to the hilt. They don't want to hear anything negative, or discuss the pros and cons of how the job is done.

The truth is that some managers like to be surrounded by "yes" people. It heightens their sense of self-importance and reassures those who are insecure that a subordinate poses no threat to their position.

When a Politician tells you that something has to be done right away, the chances are that he or she has made a commitment to higher-ups. So although the particular task may not seem very important, it's best to make it your own top priority.

If you work for an overt Politician, you'll never be in the dark about what top management is thinking, because this kind of boss sticks strictly to the party line. As long as you're a team player, a Politician type of boss will usually support you. The main danger with this type of boss is that his loyalties can change faster than tires at an Indianapolis 500 pit stop.

Office Politicians may or may not know what they're doing, but they always know how to make the right moves. They carefully conceal any weaknesses they have and play everything according to the rules of their constituency—which is top management. As long as you recognize that a boss is doing this, then you should be able to cope with it. On the other hand, if your plight is intolerable, it's best to start searching for a job somewhere else.

PRODUCING UNDER CONSTANT PRESSURE

If there's one trait that impresses a boss—or anyone else—it's the ability to respond well under pressure. Crunch-time performers are impressive, be it on the battlefield or under the gun in the world of work. Still, there are bosses that overdo it. A constant stream of pressure-packed days can be overwhelming, unless you recognize your limitations and learn how to handle the strain.

There are two main methods you can use to grapple with an overload of work. One is to learn how to fend off your boss, while the other is improving how you manage your workload. The following pointers can aid you in the latter regard:

- **Concentrate on priority assignments.** Put less important tasks on the back burner.

- **Delegate as much as possible.** Don't try to do everything yourself. Learn to let go and trust your subordinates to accept responsibility.
- **Don't put self-imposed pressures on yourself.** Everyone works best when they're relaxed and well rested.
- **Anticipate and plan ahead.** Start known projects before they're actually assigned.
- **Don't procrastinate.** Seemingly impossible jobs become less daunting the further along you are at working on them.
- **Eliminate other chores when possible.** For example, skip meetings that don't require your presence. Or stop sending written memos except when absolutely necessary.

As far as avoiding assignments in the first place, let's look at how you can counterattack when your boss is overloading you with work. Some handy tactics include

1. **Pleading poverty.** "I'm short two people this week." "One of my machines is down." "Joe's on vacation." "Marvin's out sick."
2. **Pawning it off elsewhere.** "The machines in Kate's group are more suitable for this type of job."
3. **Trading off work.** "The only way I can handle this job is if you move the Bishop order somewhere else."

NOTE: Another twist on this is to get your boss to push back completion dates on other work that you have. Be careful here, though, especially if you have a boss who tends to forget about agreements.

4. **Standing tall.** "You know I'm cooperative, but my people are overworked." "This is the fourth time in a row that my group has been given a rush job. Can't we share the wealth?"

◆ ◆ ◆ **TIP:** If you think your unit gets the lion's share of rush jobs, keep notes to prove it when you argue this point with the boss.

MAKING THE BEST OF AN INCOMPETENT BOSS

Working for an Incompetent boss can be a trying experience. Fortunately, most bosses know their job and perform it adequately. However, if you do have the misfortune to work for an ineffective boss, it's prudent to be cautious in your dealings with him/her.

Usually, Incompetents are the result of trying to put a square peg in a round hole. One of the failures of management in general is a lack of attention when placing people in management positions.

In some instances, people become managers by virtue of time on the job. Everyone else may have long since left or been promoted, so Sam Seniority gets the open slot by default. Actually, Sam may have been an excellent worker in his previous position, but just doesn't have the ability to manage people and other resources effectively.

An out-and-out Incompetent may be able to disguise his inadequacies. He may be lucky enough to have good people working for him—including you—or a friendly personality that tends to compensate for his weaknesses.

Working for an Incompetent boss may mean that you get stuck doing unnecessary work, as he bumbles his way through life. Never expect to get a direct answer—so don't waste time looking for one. Incompetent bosses can hurt you in other ways.

First of all, if you're doing a good job, they'll take all of the credit. Since they don't believe in rocking the boat, they won't push you for pay raises and promotions. They may also be prone to nitpick. This means changing something here and something there in everything you do.

The only advantage of working for an Incompetent is that it's easy to look good by comparison. However, be careful not to make an enemy by openly capitalizing on the Incompetent's lack of knowledge. After all, no one likes to be thought of as stupid.

◆ ◆ ◆ **CAUTION:** Don't be too quick to peg your boss as an Incompetent. Once in a while, someone has a boss with whom she has a personality clash. Just because personalities differ, that doesn't mean a boss is incompetent. After all, in most cases a manager had to have something on the ball to get where she is.

WORKING UNDER TYRANTS

Tyrants treat you in a high-handed, harsh, and dictatorial manner. These abusive, abrasive bosses are gluttons for power. They're even reluctant to delegate tasks because that means they can't hog all the control.

Tyrants tend to rule arbitrarily, as despots, cruelly imposing their will. Their need to feel omnipotent isn't met until they can demean you and trample upon your ego. A favorite tactic is to interrupt you in the middle of what you're saying, assassinating your character as they tear apart your remarks.

They have deluded themselves to believe that they, uniquely, know the right answers. If you criticize them, you'll escalate their attacks. You have to assert yourself with utmost tact if you are going to survive their reign.

Your goal is to get your boss to treat you in a civil, courteous manner and to stop being so overbearing. To accomplish this

1. **Prepare to act.** Stop accepting the situation. If you do nothing, the sharp stabs will fester until you finally blow up or break down.
2. **Appear firm, strong, and unemotional.** If you reveal that you're weak and angry, the Tyrant will try harder to dominate you. Let him rage. You must appear serene and not threaten his majesty's self-image.
3. **Use tact to get his attention and respect.** Telling him he's wrong will make him seek revenge. Instead, ask questions that show you want to talk. He may actually be starving for approval and affection but trying to get it the wrong way. Even a Tyrant needs a friend.

◆ ◆ ◆ **TIP:** Don't grieve—leave. Bosses who seem as tyrannical as Attila the Hun are often quite bright. Learn all you can from them. Then, if you can't change the climate and your boss is solidly entrenched, to keep your sanity, think about working someplace else.

PROTECTING YOURSELF FROM BULLIES

Bullies are habitually cruel, threatening your present and future. While Tyrants believe they were ordained to rule, Bullies believe they can control if they use hate and fear as weapons.

Bullies appear self-confident and strong because they intimidate weaker people. If you vacillate and submit, act afraid, or react with rage, that proves to them that you are inferior and deserve to be disparaged.

When Bully bosses belittle you, crushing your self-confidence with their authoritarian threats, your best defense is an offense. You have to stand up to Bullies.

Your aim is to protect your job by redeeming your self-esteem and, thereby, gaining the Bully's respect. To fight back, arm yourself with friendliness and self-confidence and avoid a clash of wills.

1. **Let the Bully vent his anger without attempting to stop him.** In a pleasant tone, pose questions to get him to disclose what's really bugging him. He may be a Bully, but he's human, so don't be surprised if he reacts positively when you show concern for his feelings.
2. **Deal with the problem without criticizing his thinking or actions.** If you agree with part of what he says, say so while indicating that some other points confuse you. If you totally disagree, show respect for his authority as you ask him to consider another possibility.

3. **Be wary about ganging up to make a complaint.** Unless this is very carefully orchestrated, if a group of you marches into his office, your boss will feel threatened. Then he'll clamp down harder. And going to the boss's boss will probably backfire, too. Your boss may be hailed in the upper echelons as an achiever deserving their total support.

♦ ♦ ♦ **TIP:** Bullies lose their power if you don't cower. Deep down, they doubt they deserve your respect. They admire your speaking with self-assurance and confidence. So when they bombard, don't counterpunch. Best the Bully with your strong, firm, courteous demeanor.

DEFUSING TIME BOMBS

Time Bombs—their anger unexpectedly erupts in tantrums. Time Bombs differ from other hostile bosses in that their actions aren't planned. Their frenzy leaves you feeling both confused and frightened because you are witnessing someone out of control.

These are adults who throw childish tantrums. They learned early in life that exploding in anger is a defense against fear and frustration.

Time Bombs can't tolerate opposing opinions. When you disagree, they believe you are criticizing them on a personal level. During a quiet discussion, if your statement happens to touch a sensitive spot, it's snap, crackle, pop. They suddenly erupt in a rage, shouting tirades, blaming you for everything. Your mind goes into shock.

Your immediate aim is to defuse the Time Bomb and then to gain his trust.

1. **Protect yourself.** While the Time Bomb is having his tantrum, if you think he may become violent, leave instantly, saying you'll talk later.
2. **Be patient.** Wait for the exploder to run down and regain some self-control. Especially don't mention the "explosive" issue. Get his attention after a few minutes by repeatedly shouting his name ("John, John, John, listen, listen.") Keep a friendly tone to avoid a screaming duet.
3. **Tactfully resume talking if he calms down.** Acknowledge his thinking. Show that you understand how important the issue is to him. Reassure him that you're on his side, that you're not questioning his authority, you're merely offering a suggestion.

♦ ♦ ♦ **TIP:** If Mount Vesuvius starts erupting in an open area, usher your boss to a quiet spot. Try to save him from embarrassing himself. Exploders need your support and understanding to help them cope with their fears. Be respectful and concerned as you gingerly attempt to disarm the Time Bomb.

WINNING RECOGNITION UNDER FAME CLAIMERS

Fame Claimers haughtily assume credit for your work. To them, this isn't stealing. They're just taking what they believe to be rightfully theirs. Sure, you did the work and you're not getting the recognition you deserve, but the boss believes he earned the credit.

These Fame Claimers are pumped up with pride they are unwilling to share. Their haughty air of self-importance advertises their belief that they alone are responsible for results because they are totally in control. If you tactfully accuse them of stealing your credit, they'll promise to arrange some recognition for you. Don't hold your breath. People who are so hungry to get credit are usually extremely touchy if you criticize them.

There's more involved here than satisfying your ego. Getting acclaimed as an idea person and a good implementer is important for your career advancement. Your objective is clear. You need to gain recognition for your achievements.

1. **Share the credit and gain a friend.** Be willing to dole out some of the acclaim. Instead of complaining that you didn't get recognition, acknowledge to the boss and everyone else around whatever you can legitimately say the boss taught you. Win over the boss by getting him to think of the two of you as a team.

2. **Share problems and how you're handling them.** Be considerate of the boss's time as you plot ways to become more visible to him on the important matters. You can ask his opinion without seeking his permission.

3. **Document your procedures and accomplishments.** Send progress reports to your boss and copies to anyone else who might possibly benefit from reading them. This written evidence has a double benefit. Many people become aware of your efforts, you get the credit you deserve, and in addition, having this record will help you recall your feats during future negotiations.

◆ ◆ ◆ **TIP:** To convert your boss from stealing your praises to singing your praises, keep telling him how much he is helping you. Your boss needs an extra boost to satisfy his greed and need for recognition, but neither of you could successfully accomplish the task alone. Both of you deserve to paste up the gold stars.

OVERCOMING IDEA BLOCKERS

Idea Blockers advance their ideas and obstruct the ones they don't originate. If it's their idea, it has enormous potential; if it's someone else's, they slash it to shreds. Idea Blocker bosses are unreasonable in the way they disagree or oppose what you're suggesting. They don't want to delegate the act of thinking to anyone else in the department. If you dare to suggest an original thought, you'll feel the tag "Troublemaker" being pinned to your lapel.

You wish your boss would plan with you, not for you. If the procedures to improve the operation are so obvious to you, why doesn't the boss want to hear any of your suggestions? You get the feeling that he resents your interference. He does.

Your goal is to get your ideas considered objectively without antagonizing your boss. This is a good time to review the way in which you are telling the boss your recommendations. Here's a short checklist. How well do you score?

Checklist for Offering Unsolicited Ideas/Proposals

- *Are you offering suggestions for the boss to consider rather than demanding changes?* All you can hope for is that your idea will be considered; the boss's role is to determine the value of the suggestion.

- *Do you make the boss feel that he had a part in the development of your idea?* Mention that this is an outgrowth of something he said last week or that the idea came to you this morning when the boss was discussing the need to increase productivity. You get him to hear you by claiming to have heard him.

- *Before plunging in, do you first ask the boss if he has a few minutes to talk to you?* Otherwise, you might catch him at a bad time. If you know you can garner peer support, and if the atmosphere at staff meetings is free and open, throw the question to the rest of the group.

- *Before you talk do you put your thoughts to paper?* By writing out your idea, you can be crystal clear and sharpen the main points that need to be brought out before you talk to your boss. If you ramble, you're wasting the boss's time.

- *Do you deal with drawbacks as well as benefits?* This is especially important when it comes to spending time, money, and other resources. When preparing a proposal, pay close attention to whatever the boss is saying on this subject, question him, and get him to restate his position. Expand your idea with ways to implement it.

- *Can you defend your plan if it's torn apart?* As the boss is talking, make note of what you consider to be his legitimate objections. When you speak again, first answer the valid criticism, ignore the rest, and then continue with other positive points.

- *Did you do your homework? Is it possible that this fantastic idea of yours was already considered and rejected? Is the regulation you want to change one that was initiated by your boss?* Protect yourself. Ask the boss what experience he has had with this sort of thing. If he started the regulation, ask how he believes the conditions have changed since then and what might be needed now to meet these changes.

- *Are you sure what you're saying is in sync with the aggressive style in which the boss paints himself?* If one of his favorite sayings is, "You have to get them before they get you." beware of suggestions the boss might resent because he should have come up with the idea himself and didn't.

- *Do you ask the boss how long before he might have a decision?* Leave the door open by getting him to tell you when to check back with him.

- *Do you give a new boss time to size up the operation?* He may be refusing all suggestions from you and your colleagues in an effort to appear confident when he doesn't feel like he's in command. Don't say anything yet. You may no longer have a problem with him once he gets his bearings.

◆ ◆ ◆ **TIP:** Without kowtowing, you can build up the boss instead of tearing him down. If he's in good standing with the company, ask yourself why he remains there. He must be doing something top management likes. Learn what it is. Gain strength by exercising your tact and feeding his ego.

GETTING STRAIGHT ANSWERS FROM HYPOCRITES

Hypocrites are two-faced double-dealers who purposely misrepresent or mislead you. Hypocrite bosses are sneaky. You can't trust them. They pretend to be your good buddy, but you have to find out through the company grapevine that the program you direct has been cut out of next year's budget. Or the boss cons you into confiding in him and then uses the information against you. Another favorite tactic of Hypocrites is to take facts and figures out of context or to quote nonexistent studies and authorities. Led astray, you draw incorrect conclusions.

The only thing you can depend on from Hypocrite bosses is that they will actually do the opposite of what they pretend to be doing.

Your goal is to get a straight answer from you boss so that you know where you stand and can plan accordingly. Before you assume that the boss is out to get you, you need to find out what's making him act that way.

1. **Ask questions that require direct answers.** The boss probably doesn't realize that he has wronged you or hurt you. He may have been thinking out loud when he spoke to you. It may have sounded definite to you and inconclusive to him. But as a result, the great expectations he built you up for led to a letdown. Although he was proceeding along a direct route, he was indeed insensitive to your feelings.

2. **Protect yourself in the future.** Don't accept anything your boss tells you at face value until it's confirmed in writing or announced in front of other people. If he asks you to keep a plan secret, honor this request, but ask when you may inquire if the plan will be enacted. Once you are convinced that the boss has made a definite deal with you, publicize it, involving other people, so that he will have difficulty backing out. You can, for example, prepare a memo stating your understanding of what is to occur. Give the original to the boss, keep a copy for yourself, and send copies to others who in *any* way will be involved.

♦ ♦ ♦ **TIP:**   Find some goals on which you agree. The boss you see as a hypocritical snake in the grass may actually be a fraidy-cat who has a tiger by the tail. He pussyfoots, lacking courage to tell you face to face that he decided on changes because a situation became more difficult than anticipated. You're not the only one who's been victimized by such behavior. Even some Presidents of the United States were reputed to be similarly gutless when communicating bad news to subordinates. Understand your boss's flaw and work around it.

DEFENDING YOURSELF AGAINST RIDICULERS

Ridiculers belittle you with taunting wit that scarcely covers their true intent. Some rude bosses use sarcasm to thinly veil their criticism. They mistakenly think this brand of humor makes it easier for you to accept a correction. But you don't sense any jokes coming across. You just feel sharp barbs. You try to laugh when you really want to hide and sulk.

Other bosses pretend to be teasing you in order to hide their impatience, saying things like "Only my addled ninety-year-old grandfather would take so much time to get me this information."

Good-natured teasing you can take. Criticism about your work you can handle. But these bosses taunt and humiliate you with personal attacks, especially in front of other people. To you, the implication is clear—he's telling the immediate world that he thinks you're an imbecile.

You sense that the boss is sending you a message through his sarcasm. Your objective is to get the boss to become more straightforward in telling you what he wants done and how he wants it done.

1. **Schedule a private meeting with the boss.** Be up front in admitting that you feel disturbed and want to clear the air. Do not criticize the boss for ridiculing you. Be professional and matter-of-fact so that you don't sound like a crybaby.

2. **Ask the boss to explain what he meant by the remarks.** Open the door to receive good, constructive comments. Don't make excuses for yourself. Just listen and promise to improve.

♦ ♦ ♦ **TIP:** Often bosses who utilize humor to correct or criticize their workers see themselves as standup comics. Unless you indicate otherwise, they will keep thinking that their sarcasm is a well-received way to soften an attack.

GAINING ATTENTION FROM BRUSH-OFFS

Brush-off bosses curtly dismiss you. They are too busy to answer your questions or supply what you need. Why are these bosses too busy for you? They may not admit it even to themselves, but that's the way they want it. They get bogged down in tasks that others should be doing. Not only are they unwilling to get you the help you need, they also keep others from assisting you. Brush-off bosses have trouble delegating. For one thing, they believe they can do everything better than everybody else.

Another reason is the fear that if they build up their staff and let go of some of the tasks, others will no longer regard them as vital to the operation. As a result, they stifle their own growth. They leave themselves no time to plan important future moves, and they leave you feeling frustrated.

Your objective is to complete the jobs you've been assigned. That includes extracting necessary data from a busy boss.

1. **Punt—don't confront.** If you tell the boss he's wrong, he has to defend his ego with a counterattack. So don't even give the appearance of arguing with him. Often you can turn the ball over to the boss just by inquiring about his opinion or asking him to make a choice.
2. **Focus on his needs, not yours.** You lose ground if you complain. Force yourself to totally ignore his curt manner and talk instead about the options he has for enhancing his reputation or achieving his objectives. He's more apt to help you if he views the action as helping himself. Your positive suggestions can light the way.

♦ ♦ ♦ **TIP:** You look better when you help your boss look good. Egotistical bosses worry about how their supervisors and colleagues perceive their professionalism. Give them ideas that they can claim as their own: "I thought about this yesterday when you were discussing cost-saving procedures. . . ."

LOOSENING UP INFLEXIBLE BOSSES

Inflexibles are iron-willed bosses who won't listen to others, sticking tenaciously to their ideas. They are in charge and don't you dare forget it. Their way is the only way because they say so. They rigorously and intolerantly impose unreasonable strictness.

Don't complain to these bosses if this inflexibility causes you any difficulty. They don't want to hear why it would help you if, just this once, they'd make an exception. Their rigidity is unshakable; their resolve seemingly can't be curved, bent, or diverted. Your problems won't influence them to modify their views. They suddenly can't hear what you're saying, no matter how pointed your comment. They're too busy worrying about keeping control.

Your goal is to get your obstinate boss to let a friendly, fresh but critical breeze flow over his policies and precedents. To achieve more open discussions, try these tactics

1. **Understand where the boss is coming from.** In presenting your ideas, focus on management's concerns. Explain how your proposal meets the objectives the boss is always talking about. Point up probable consequences if the idea is not accepted.

2. **Explain the mutual benefits.** Explain the benefits not only for the boss and the company but also for you. Let the boss see how eager you are for this plan to work. Show your willingness to knock yourself out to make it succeed.

3. **Acknowledge costs and obstacles.** If applicable, prepare a budget and list staffing suggestions. Explain how you'd overcome anticipated roadblocks.

4. **Go in the back door by creating the market.** Begin by documenting demand, asking opinions from those who'd be using your product or service. When users become caught up with your idea, suggest how they can help you persuade your boss to bring it about.

◆ ◆ ◆ **TIP:** If your boss won't bend, reshape your request and repeat it. People refuse for one reason and agree for another. When bosses are determined to maintain the status quo by practicing thought control, help change their minds by pulling with them instead of against them. Tap into the potential of product/service users by getting them to change the boss's mind for you. Although you've violated no rule, should your boss accuse you of being aggressive, apologize. It's easier to say you're sorry afterward than to get permission from an iron-willed autocrat beforehand.

HANDLING MEAT GRINDERS

Meat Grinders are overly candid. Their cutting criticism rips you to shreds. This time it *was* your fault. There's no way to hide this blunder that may blow your career chances. Panic takes over. Meanwhile the boss, always a stern Dutch uncle, is furious and unrelenting with his sharp accusations. But this time he has every right to be angry.

Don't answer the charges. Freeze in your tracks. Say, "I'll be right back" and leave the room or hang up the phone. Now take a few deep breaths and remember that everybody makes mistakes. It's how you face up to them that determines your future. Also keep in mind that bosses have the right to criticize your work, but that doesn't include the right to inflict cruel and unusual punishment to your ego.

Your goal is to immediately remedy your mistake and get back in the boss's good graces.

1. **Admit your error quickly and emphatically.** As soon as you realize that you, or someone under you goofed, claim the blame. In the boss's mind, this computes as, "Aha, he sees I was right to criticize him, so I suppose he's not so dumb after all. Let's see what else he has to say." Denying your mistake only makes you appear spineless; delaying causes you unnecessary hardship.

2. **Give no alibi or excuse.** If your subordinate was the one who pulled the boner, you still have to accept the responsibility. Get to the point without cushioning the misdeed. You were wrong. You are sorry. An alibi would only make the boss madder because it implies the boss accused you unjustly.

3. **Offer a way to make it better.** Suggest a plan to correct the error. Restate your boss's criticism, transforming each negative into a positive objective. If after having time to calm down, the boss continues hurling insults at you, hold on to your dignity by proclaiming that you accept the criticism as sound, but his being unnecessarily rough is delaying progress in working things out.

4. **Seek agreement on the plan.** Whatever you two come up with, be sure you're in accord before you leave. Bringing someone else in to clean up your dirty work won't improve your relationship with your boss.

◆ ◆ ◆ **TIP:** Stop predicting doomsday because you made a mistake. Everybody does. The real danger is in compounding the error by avoiding saying you're sorry or by apologizing too late.

GETTING COMMITMENTS FROM AN INDECISIVE BOSS

Certain bosses are simply unable to make decisions. If you try to get a commitment out of them, you get the old, "We'll talk about it later." The trouble is that "later" never comes. What can you do?

Short of getting another job, you have to force the issue when you have a boss who consistently avoids making decisions. Let's look at how Agnes corners her boss Paul, who is known for this trait.

Agnes: Paul, I need this requisition signed off for personnel to start the hiring process for that vacancy I have.

Paul: Let's talk about that later Agnes.

Agnes: I need to have it down to Personnel today so they can place a help-wanted ad in next Sunday's newspaper.

Paul: Just leave it on my desk. I'll get to it later.

Agnes: I need it by 10:00 A.M.

Paul: No sweat. Just put it in my box. [At 10:20 A.M., Agnes returns to Paul's office.]

Agnes: Paul, is that requisition signed?

Paul: Gee Agnes, I haven't gotten to it yet.

Agnes: Well Peggy in Personnel called looking for it. Incidentally, Mr. Trumbell [Paul's boss] was asking me if I was going to make my production quota for the quarter. I told him it wasn't likely unless we filled the vacancy I have within the next two weeks.

Paul: Oh yeah. What did he say then?

Agnes: He asked me what the delay was.

Paul: What did you tell him?

Agnes: Oh, no problem. I said there wasn't any and that you were signing off this morning so I could hand-carry the request to Personnel. He just said, "Great!"

Paul: Well, we better get it down there. Let me sign that right now.

Although it's not generally recommended to put your boss on the spot, if you have an Indecisive boss, the best method for getting action is to present him with an alternative that's worse than taking the action you seek. And that's precisely what Agnes did here.

♦ ♦ ♦ **TIP:** Don't automatically assume that your boss is indecisive just because you get a "Wally the Waffler" response such as, "I don't know . . . What do you think?" A boss who does this isn't necessarily indecisive. He may just respect your judgment and/or know that you are better able to make a decision on the subject under discussion.

BYPASSING A BOTTLENECK BOSS

In the ordinary course of events, it's improper to deliberately bypass your boss except for unusual conditions dictated by necessity. Even so, you may have a boss so totally indecisive that it's impossible to operate through normal channels.

For example, suppose you have a boss who is just coasting toward retirement and won't make a decision on anything. How do you work around him without getting yourself in trouble?

The best time to work around your boss is when he isn't in. So when your boss is out, put everything else on the back burner and concentrate on tasks that would ordinarily require your boss's approval.

Unfortunately, this kind of opportunity doesn't present itself often. That means you'll have to learn how to outmaneuver your boss on a regular basis. As a general rule, see your boss's boss (or whoever else you would secure approval from) when your boss is off somewhere at a meeting, lunch, or hovering over someone else.

The best excuse for doing this is always an urgent task that requires immediate resolution. To be successful at bypassing your boss, it's also necessary to build good rapport with the managers you'll be dealing with.

◆ ◆ ◆ **CAUTION:** Never belittle your boss to other managers. They're savvy enough to know why you're circumventing the chain of command without your filling them in on the specifics. In those instances when someone asks, "Why didn't Joe (your boss) approve this?" make an excuse such as "It's a priority and he's at a meeting."

If your boss notices that you're bypassing him, be casual and ready with an excuse. Try some of the following:

Boss: Fred, I didn't see the defects report.

You: Mr. Arsenault [his boss] was looking for it and you were at a meeting, so I gave it to him directly.

Boss: Where's the monthly production report? I don't remember signing off.

You: I sent it to Mr. Arsenault last Friday. You were out that day.

Boss: Fred, I'm not sure I'm seeing everything I should before it leaves the department.

You: Gee boss, the only time I go direct to someone else is when you're not around.

Boss: Fred, you're not keeping me posted as much as you should.

You: Sorry boss, but I know how busy you are, and I don't like to bother you with the nickel-and-dime stuff.

Obviously, how successful you are at bypassing your boss depends to a large degree on whether or not the boss takes issue with your operating procedure. If he insists on seeing everything, then for the most part you'll have to comply.

◆ ◆ ◆ **WARNING:** If you find it virtually impossible to circumvent a Bottleneck Boss, and problems develop because he holds things up, make sure he isn't using you as the Scapegoat. Casually let people know that what they are looking for was completed by you and given to your boss. Do this without being vindictive. The purpose isn't to knock your boss but rather to protect yourself from unjustified blame because of the boss's procrastination.